# REMEMBERSHIP

*New Thinking for*
*Tomorrow's Membership Organization*

## KYLE J. SEXTON

*Electronic edition available compliments of*
*ChamberMaster at RemembershipBook.com*

This publication is designed to provide accurate and authoritative information in regard to the subject matter covered. It is sold with the understanding that the publisher and author are not engaged in rendering legal, accounting, or other professional advice. If legal advice or other expert assistance is required, the services of a competent professional should be sought.

*REMEMBERSHIP*
*New Thinking for Tomorrow's Membership Organization*

First Edition | ISBN: 978-0-9835703-0-1

Published by IncPlant – *Where Ideas Go to Grow*
Salem, Oregon | IncPlant.com

Copyright © 2011 by Kyle J. Sexton

Unattributed quotations are by Kyle J. Sexton
Design and composition by Kyle J. Sexton
Cover design by Kyle J. Sexton
Cover Artwork Copyright © iStock by Saul Herrera
Edited by Jessica Chambers

Printed in the United States of America
by Your Town Press, Salem, Oregon, a member of The Salem Area Chamber of Commerce since 1974

For bulk discounts or other resources,
visit www.remembershipbook.com
or call 1-888-899-8374

*~ For Wyatt ~*

*Great things can happen*

*when you work hard*

*on something that you love,*

*for something that you love,*

*because of someone who you love.*

# Contents

# Preface

**Your membership development strategy is out of date.**

I've been saying it in speeches, chats, conversations, emails, and on and on. Are you finally getting it? Why are you hearing me, but not your members?

Eighty percent of your members don't show up for anything, yet you still tout participation as the best way to get value from membership. Unless your membership organization is a health club, you're dead wrong. The best way your members will get value from their membership is by you building a member services menu that provides them value, even if they choose to sit on their proverbial butts.

You tell members and prospects that your organization is valuable, yet you don't put a value on anything. In fact, you give away too much and charge too little. Are you really going to allow your most time-consuming members (the ones you want to fire) to pay the least amount in dues?

There is something awry in the world of membership organizations when your members are starting to detach from your association and start their own thing.

You have no advantage of proximity. Your members who work next door to each other would still rather send an email or Facebook message than meet up for coffee. So why would it be that your local association is safe from borderless threats?

Technology has never been more affordable, but your board still says "next year" for that association software purchase you've been putting off far too long.

If you are not an employee, board member, or high-level volunteer of a chamber of commerce or business-focused association, this book is not for you. If you can't imagine your organization without its sacred cow parade, pageant or pancake feed, this book is not for you.

Many of today's membership organizations are living on yesterday's bread while your members drink tomorrow's wine. If your members are putting up with it now, they won't for long.

This book is about renewing your membership development strategies because your memberships may be worthless.

## Patty Mooney is still fired up.

Her husband and business partner, Mark Schulze, was a finalist for "Most Admired CEO" by the University Club in San Diego. The announcement came a month before the event, so Patty and Mark of Crystal Pyramid, Inc. got a room at a Symphony Towers to make the event even more memorable. What an honor to be nominated.

They made their RSVP for the banquet, and just to be sure, Patty verbally confirmed with the organizers when she attended another University Club function.

About an hour before the dinner, they went to let the organizer know that one of their nominees had arrived. According to Patty, "That's when the bomb dropped."

"Oh, you're not on the list," said the organizer. "But don't worry. We'll accommodate you."

Members like to be recognized. They like to be appreciated and acknowledged. So you can imagine how dismayed Mark and Patty were as they sat at what Patty describes as the "kiddy table, like the one in the basement on Thanksgiving Day."

Can we get a do-over in this story?

Clubs which rely on events for contact with their members could – and should – have some parachutes in place just in case the plane starts to sputter.

One such parachute could be to reserve seats at the banquet for the staff of the University Club (and their guests) at some of the best tables in the house. The organizer could have said, "I'm sorry, I'm not finding your table assignment. You two must be at a very special table."

Special indeed. The staff, whose job it is to make members happy, has just done their job by giving up their seat to the member.

I'll never forget this quote from Mike McLaran, CEO of the Salem (Oregon) Area Chamber of Commerce, and my mentor: "If we make a mistake, the affected member hits the lottery."

At first glance, this approach seems to put the member at the center of the action. But think about it: this philosophy empowers the staff organizer to deliver some very good news to that member.

Now the staff can feel like Ed McMahon with a big check and a big smile.

Yes, I think a do-over is in order.

It's too bad this club is now of less value to Patty and Mark. While the nomination was still very impressive, their lousy experience will always be the first thing they remember. It could have been different.

The do-over illustrates how businesses with intangible products can create a lasting, tangible impact on their members. Tangible, like the letter Patty wrote to a San Diego magazine about the experience, which eventually made its way to my inbox.

When people are happy they might tell someone. When they are unhappy they tell ten. Well, maybe that was true in the 1990s.

Now it's more like thousands, thanks to virtual friends, social networks, blogs, email lists, list-serves, digital publishing and the like.

## That's Not a Membership Organization, or Is It?

United Airlines did a number on me once. After arriving at Portland International Airport more than an hour before my flight was to depart, I watched in awe and angst as a staff of five United Airlines folks took twenty minutes to assist ten people in front of me with their check-in. It was a jumbled mess.

As I swiped my card to check in 43 minutes before my departure, my reservation could not be retrieved by the automated check-in station, so I politely waited. After a minute or so, I asked for help and was directed to the back of a line of six customers with one agent re-booking them.

"I don't need to be re-booked, Ma'am. I just need to be checked in. My flight doesn't leave for another forty minutes."

"You need to wait in that line and our agent will re-book you. I'm not authorized to check you in," she said. Hmm.

Twenty more minutes go by before I get to talk to the agent and she immediately starts to re-book me. "Ma'am," I begged. "My flight doesn't leave for another twenty minutes. Can you just check me in?"

"Sir," she huffed in her most annoyed tone. I could tell I was about to be lectured. "You should have checked in forty-five minutes before your flight. Why were you late?"

"I wasn't late, Ma'am. I got in line an hour before my departure time. Is there any way you can check me in? I really need to be in Los Angeles today."

"You can talk to my supervisor. She's over there." So I went.

I wait for sixty seconds as the supervisor musters up the tolerance to acknowledge my presence. "Yes," she drones.

"Hello," I said using my sweetest, not-irritated voice. "Your agent wants to re-book me but I just want to get on my flight. Could you check me in, please?"

"You should've been here 45 minutes before your flight. Why were you late." (Most questions end in question marks, hers did not.)

"I stood in this line for an extraordinary amount of time," I explained.

"No, you didn't. Get back in that line and she'll re-book you."

Why do I share this story of United Airlines with you, since they are not a membership organization?

Membership isn't just a business plan; it can also be a service philosophy.

While it's true that I'm not a member of United Airlines in any way, I do feel that I am a member of Delta Airlines. I love Delta. They do all the little things for me that United won't. Delta is nice. They communicate with me in a respectful and kind way at every turn.

I've logged almost 250,000 domestic miles with Delta, and they haven't changed the way they treat me in that entire time. The perks are better, but they aren't any nicer to me because I'm a Silver, Gold, Platinum or Diamond Member.

The day United Airlines made me feel insignificant, I ended up having a pleasant flight on Alaska Airlines. I bought a new one-way ticket for $300, and I'm hoping to get that amount of satisfaction by including that story here.

You could write a book, too, and share your own stories. Perhaps it will be better than therapy. But once you do this to your own members, there is not enough therapy in the world.

*Every day, membership organizations are having little, tiny 'United Airlines moments' with their members. After a while, these moments add up to organizational irrelevance.*

*Disclaimer:* I've had plenty of my own United Airlines moments. Once, I forgot to call back a member of almost thirty years. With my tail between my legs, I went to his office to apologize.

It's easy to tell when you're talking to an old-school businessman: there is no computer in his office, just a phone. The one thing I know of old school businessmen is they don't want excuses. He didn't need to remind me that he has been a member for decades, but he did. Of course, he was right to mention it.

My point in sharing this is that you're not always going to get it right. In fact, there will be times when you get it completely wrong with the member who deserves it least, but the spirit in which you approach the situation—or fix it—matters.

## Get Something, or Get Something Done

Mick Fleming is the President and CEO of the American Chamber of Commerce Executives, a professional association for chamber professionals, and has been in the association business for a few decades. Mick suggests there are two types of members in an organization: "Those who want to get something, and those who want to get something done."

I find that there is a difference in longevity among members who simply want to get something. Once they get it, they are more inclined to leave. Mission accomplished.

If you don't engage them with features of your organization that will entice them to stick around and "get something more," you lose them.

Unfortunately, there is no map for this.

## On Mission, Vision and Function

A much more challenging membership-based business organization might be one like the International Hotel & Restaurant Association. Their members are mostly national hotel and restaurant associations.

Confused yet? Their members have members of their own. To further complicate the issue, their members do not have the luxury of having locality, demography, geography, or even language in common with each other. The function of an organization like IH&RA is complicated by these issues.

On the other hand, the core functions of a chamber of commerce are pretty straight forward, according to the Western Association of Chamber Executives:

Strengthen the local economy
Represent business interests with governments
Take political action and develop leaders
Promote the community
Provide networking opportunities

Has your membership organization determined your core functions?

Different than your mission statement, vision statement, or unique selling proposition, your core functions are how your members, and the public, will measure your performance.

Think of your association as a college course. What would be contained in your syllabus? If there are definable stages in the business life of your members, how many syllabi will it take to cover your core functions?

Chambers of commerce have five, but some chambers of commerce also serve a tourism function in their city or town. That could be covered under "promoting the community" for obvious reasons, but tourism is probably more appropriately labeled as "strengthening the local economy."

# Lessons in Loyalty

"The benefits of a membership association can only be attained and realized if you are an active participant," writes John Rudy, the head of Tasty Catering. "The decision to remain a member ultimately depends on the return on investment both from a fiscal and emotional standpoint. Neither can be achieved if you are not an active member."

Tasty Catering's staff is encouraged to attend meetings and participate so they can decide if a particular association is a good fit for them.

"Our staff has remained loyal to those associations where their contributions are recognized, they have fun and feel as though they are networking with those who they enjoy, admire and learn from," he added. If your membership organization is struggling with member retention, I think it's worthwhile to read that statement again.

Rudy made it clear that he only sees a return on investment when his people are involved in a social experience. In my experience, this feeling is over-emphasized in most membership organizations.

# Networking, Not-working, and Full-Contact Sales

I had the chance to facilitate a focus group at an American Chamber of Commerce Executives Convention. This panel consisted of four members of the Greater Raleigh Chamber of Commerce. When I asked how I could position my chamber as a favorable investment for a business owner, two of the panelists responded similarly.

Summarizing: "Don't talk to us about networking. When you say 'networking,' we think 'full-contact sales,' and we don't have time to subject ourselves to salespeople or business owners who are more concerned with selling me something than connecting with me as a peer."

John Rudy agrees where his Tasty team is concerned. "Those associations and groups where constant peddling of wares by members occurs are not conducive to growth and are dropped quickly as it is more about self-serving results than the goals of the group.

"We have terminated memberships in associations when there is a feeling that contributions have been taken advantage of, taken for granted, or ignored," Rudy said. "This has been compounded by groups that are not organized effectively and meetings haphazard and irregular. Associations with leadership and members who push to achieve personal agendas and financial rewards are other reasons we have decided to not renew memberships in associations."

Avery Horzewski of AVE Consulting agrees. She is a member of Women in Consulting, a San Francisco Bay Area professional organization.

"I really dislike networking, and find it uncomfortable," states Horzewski. "But Women in Consulting (WIC) meetings are so unlike any other organization's events that I've attended. From the very beginning, I met other consultants who were willing to answer any questions that I had about running a consulting business.

"Women in Consulting has also provided me with a close group of colleagues to whom I can turn to for specific advice, like a board of advisers really. Whether it's how to handle a sticky client situation, review a client proposal, or offer advice about a new business direction, they're *always* willing to share their insights—and I do the same for them. Many people look at what I do as a very solitary profession—but that's not the case. My WIC colleagues, many of whom are now also good friends, are just that—colleagues."

# Words Mean Things

The difference for Avery is that Women in Consulting is not considered networking. She associates networking with discomfort, like most of the world. Women in Consulting are her peers, her friends. I wondered about how Women in Consulting promotes the value of membership, so I nosed in on their website to see. As I suspected, the word "networking" is only found in three obscure places on their web site. "Network," however, is used in places where you would otherwise find "networking."

A network is something you build, where networking is an activity. The gulf between these two words is growing daily. Building a network is something every business must do, but networking can be replaced with advertising or other functions of marketing.

Associations which focus on building connections or network development instead of "networking" are not only teaching members how to talk about them, but they are differentiating themselves from the masses of "networking" opportunities.

People are suspicious of professional networkers. We often feel like we'll be pitched something at some point in the relationship. Professional networkers are sketchy; you're not sure what they do. Perhaps they are job-hoppers, never staying in one job for too long.

Networking is a catch-all term, but I think this word should only apply in cases where people are meeting each other for the first time.

Most chambers of commerce have a morning or evening networking event. These events attract the usual suspects, so networking usually takes a back seat to catching up with friends. After all, why would you choose discomfort over satisfying? Perhaps events like these aren't really networking.

  **REMEMBER:** Evaluate each of your regularly scheduled events and programs to determine whether they are networking (meeting new people) or network development (building relationships). If it's network development, stop calling it networking.

## Public Speaking, Death, and Networking

Kathleen Watson is a business networking strategist and author of *Net Profit: Business Networking Without the Nerves.* She's qualified to comment in this area for more reasons than one. Watson's experience with some chambers of commerce wasn't so pleasant.

"At one particular chamber event, I was ignored for over two minutes while trying to enter a conversation," wrote Watson in an email. "At a member orientation for another chamber, one of the chamber ambassadors leaned away from me to whisper something in another veteran member's ear."

I can relate to Kathleen, here. Before I came to work for the Salem Area Chamber of Commerce, I was a member of several chambers throughout Oregon. Though most who know me now would find this hard to believe, I was an introvert, and nervous around large groups. I think most people are.

If I hadn't been introduced around by one of my co-workers at a chamber function for the first couple of times attending, it would have found it a very intimidating scenario.

On one hand, it's a good thing that all of your members know each other and enjoy each others' company.

On the other hand, it's regrettable to find a sizable social gap at your events between those who are new and those who have been around for a while.

The Ambassador program to which Kathleen refers is a popular way for organizations to formalize a system to acclimate new members. It's doubly unfortunate in this case that Kathleen's negative experience comes at the hands of someone whose function should make her more comfortable.

It makes me wonder how many members have been lost by associations for reasons like Kathleen Watson's. I'm sure I'm not the only membership director who has suspected social foul play as a cause for losing a possible long-term member.

Whispers and cold shoulders are kryptonite to grace and hospitality.

"At the only chamber of which I'm still a member," adds Watson, "there's an outstanding mix of friendliness and professionalism. I've been a member of this Chamber for nearly 10 years. My annual dues are pretty much a no-brainer investment for me."

# I'll Have Some Grace with My Membership, Please

The painful experience described by Kathleen Watson calls for an intervention from Shawna Schuh. Shawna is a Certified Speaking Professional and author of several books. My favorite is *How to Nail Voice Mail*, but her *Business Graces* book and website (BusinessGraces.com) are an excellent ruler by which to measure your politeness acumen.

Shawna says if you want to be viewed as gracefully hospitable (rather than stuffy, snobby or cliquish), simply act like the host. Basic, right?

Common sense – and my mother – would tell you to never whisper around other people. Secrets are rude. People's feelings are most often hurt by the worst case scenario in their mind, not actual events.

*If you and your organization foster an environment where whispering is tolerated and cliques are rewarded, your days are numbered. Or, perhaps, you're an invitation-only social club.*

# Participation versus Partnership

The membership business model tends to undervalue individual benefits because most functions of the organization are included in a membership package. For items which aren't included, the assumption is that you'll have reduced rates for members, whereas non-members pay retail rates.

Too often, when new features to membership are added, they are essentially given away. The thinking here is that these one or two new benefits will attract enough new members to justify giving it away to all.

This is a race to the bottom, and I would bet you'll get there. If this describes your membership organization, you're not alone.

Event-related benefits provide an experience for participants, generally lending a different flavor to your brand. There's a culture at each event based on who is there, and how it may be different than the last event.

The success of association mixers with open or structured networking depends on whether your event is peer-to-peer or shark-to-prey.

The popularity of your gala event will depend on the quality of the food and the overall "fun factor".

And the brand of your organization will depend on whether your members attend events because they are productive and meaningful, or because they feel guilty for missing them.

Guilt is a funny thing. Many associations are good at guilt. If you think you're not, let's make sure.

If you've ever said, "You get out of our association what you put into it," you may be good at guilt.

If you've ever said, "Join, get involved, and your business will grow," you may be good at guilt.

If you've ever told someone, "I haven't seen you at any meetings lately," then you're *pretty good* at guilt.

The problem isn't that you're really good at events; it's your assumption that what is valuable to *you* will be valuable to *them*. Your membership organization's value is subjective.

In your race to the bottom, you've added membership benefits which serve the squeaky wheels. You may have artificially inflated the value of showing up for events in a time when your competition is looking for fewer things to do, not more.

Your competition includes networking groups, little league and charitable organizations. Any function of your target's life which they love more than you is competition.

"But what if we're just not that remarkable?" you wonder. You are replaceable, probably upon receiving the next renewal invoice.

*Are you really prepared for every one of your members to show up for your meeting or event? If not, stop inviting everyone. The days of the cattle-call are long gone.*

If your organization exists for the advocacy of business, industry, or social cause, align your features and functions accordingly.

## Health Club Memberships

I spent five years in marketing and advertising for health clubs. I learned that there are two types of sales presentations: museum tours, and needs-analysis.

The museum tour starts with, "Let me show you around." Needs-analysis begins with, "Why are you here?"

Too many business-focused organizations are giving museum tours of membership features instead of asking the more important question, "Why are you here?" Or even better, "What's keeping you up at night?" We'll come back to that one.

Health clubs sell memberships which require that you show up in order to benefit. In my five years, I never had a member who complained about a membership for which they never showed up.

To put it another way, members' expectations for results depend on them coming to the gym, and they accept this responsibility on their part.

The predicament for business associations comes when you realize you've been selling health club memberships to your business association.

## Seven Dirty Words for Membership Organizations

Comedian George Carlin had the seven dirty words you can't say on television. I have the seven dirty words you can't say in the chamber of commerce business.

You get out what you put in.

Said another way: Return on involvement. You get out of it what you put into it. Join, get involved and your business will grow. Nothing could be further from the truth.

I hear these phrases in conferences, staff meetings and board rooms of chambers of commerce and associations across North America.

The Western Association of Chamber Executives conducted a study, the results of which make up the WACE Toolkit. Sixty-eight percent of respondents indicated they haven't joined the chamber because they don't have time to participate.

They weren't given a sales pitch as part of this study, so why do they think they *have to* participate?

Here's why: participation, as defined by attending meetings and events, is so ingrained in the image of chambers of commerce that this was the number one reason for not joining. Regardless of context, this is a problem which needs to be solved.

If your association's core functions include representing the interests of your industry, neighborhood, community, or market sector, then your membership has benefited from your existence long before they became members.

The primary value of your organization does not rely on your function—it relies on your purpose. How well you fulfill, communicate and report on your purpose is another story altogether.

Your functions, events, programs and initiatives are a secondary reason for joining; however, because they are much easier to promote, they have become your primary selling proposition.

Advocacy is much more difficult to convey. If you weren't there, it's more difficult to sell your history. This is why effective organizational management becomes more effective the longer it stays in place.

There is an exponential increase in performance over the long term when the right team is in place.

## You're Not Listening

Sixty-eight percent of people say they don't have time to participate, but you keep beating that drum. Perhaps you've gained that reputation by rewarding only the people who show up for things. The photos you put in your newsletters and marketing are taken at your events and programs.

Ten percent say they don't join because they don't do business locally. Do they think you are Main Street organizations? Are you? Should you be something more? Answer these questions, then ask your staff and board to answer this, as well.

If you decide you are something more, act on it. Be deliberate in every single way. Don't just say that you're a multi-faceted business organization—be one.

For years, you've been teaching your members to drop their membership when what you provide to them works. Maybe you should read that again.

*Join the chamber, get involved and your business will grow.* So, they join, they get involved and their business grows. Then what? If it worked, now they don't have time to network because they are tending to their growing business, so they drop their membership.

If it works, if membership does what you said it would do, there's nothing more for them. "Thank you, membership organization! It worked, so now I'm leaving. Don't get me wrong; I'm satisfied, I'm just not that loyal."

You have been using guilt to get your members to come to events and programs in order to receive value. So, each time your member receives an invoice for membership dues, they feel guilty (all over again) for not taking your advice, for not coming to your meetings, for not being comfortable with networking, for not using their membership the way you teach them they ought to.

You've told them they are not an ideal member. They aren't your favorite. You reward all the ones who come to meetings, and that's all. The only photos you promote are ones taken at your events, and they are of the cool kids.

# If Pricing is the Chicken, Value is the Egg

Reid Neubert and some other members were unhappy with the direction and business practices of a San Francisco professional association, so they started their own. The Council of Business Advisors is an association of trusted advisors to business.

According to Neubert, Council members are experienced professionals who are well-regarded in their fields and have a high level of competency in their respective areas of expertise. They serve primarily executives and the owners/managers of businesses.

I asked Reid what caused the riff with the other organization. He said this:

"They raised their already high annual dues by fifty percent to $1200, which we felt was much too high, and weren't sure we were getting any value added for the increase. After much consideration, I spearheaded starting our own organization taking what we felt was most valuable from their model and brainstorming ways to make it as valuable as possible to our members."

# The Quirks of Membership Organizations

Many business structures are remarkable precisely because they are quirky or difficult. Membership organizations shouldn't be this way, in my opinion, but there are some companies who have capitalized on bizarre access strategies in the marketplace.

Starbucks recognizes that standing in line is part of the brand experience. This provides the reasoning behind their late adoption of drive-through-windows and limiting the number of cash registers, no matter how large the café.

Wireless phone companies make exclusive deals with service providers in order to get the most marketing exposure for their premium products. Sure, Apple could have sold more iPhones by cutting deals with both AT&T and Verizon upon launching, but AT&T offered the sweeter marketing package. Until Verizon inked a deal with Apple two years later, you had to endure changing service providers in order to get the phone you wanted.

In this case, difficult and complex are in the business plan.

As much as these examples make it complicated to do business with these companies, they are hoping – no, banking – that they will keep you longer because of it.

Wireless companies know it is a hassle to change. Starbucks knows that waiting is inconvenient, but it seems okay because they attract a customer who doesn't mind being seen in line at Starbucks. Some brand experts argue that Starbucks customers *want to be seen in line* at Starbucks.

Many online service providers know that if they charge a monthly service fee, you will weigh the hassle of cancelling against the low cost of the service (which you may not use enough to justify the service).

At Gold's Gym, we weren't this way. Other franchisees in urban centers would charge a ridiculously low amount, say, $19 per month, in the hopes that the customer would keep the membership months or years longer instead of initiating the cancellation.

About three-quarters of chambers of commerce charge for dues based on how many employees are in a business. You tell them how many employees your business has and they tell you how much your dues will be. I never liked this system.

This is a lazy way to build a business or membership organization. Members who pay $1,000 per year are getting the same benefits as the member who pays $300.

Whoever came up with this strategy surely was not a large employer, and possibly not a capitalist.

In a sluggish economy, consumers re-evaluate the value proposition of their business relationships. In April of 2008, as gas prices nearly doubled within a month, retailers complained that consumers stopped spending money, when, in fact, they were just adjusting personal budgets.

About that same time, the Salem Chamber was in its second year of a tiered dues membership structure, and boy were we glad.

As businesses were adjusting to their customers' adjustment, they had a little extra time to wheel and deal with their vendors. The 12 months following the fuel price-doubling would prove to be an historic economic crisis for Americans.

Michael Dalby, CEO of One Southern Indiana, once told me he is "the poster child for changing to tiered dues in a down economy."

One Southern Indiana initiated their tiered dues program as the financial meltdown swept the country.

A year later, the organization had fewer members and more revenue.

It hardly seems possible. Even after business closures caused an unusual amount of lost members, membership organizations have gained in membership revenue by offering their members a choice in investment, a choice in value, and a choice in status.

Businesses which offer more value for higher investments will most easily appreciate the strategy behind membership tiers.

## When the Message is Clear, the Money Comes Easy.

When a chamber says they have a member retention problem, they may actually have a sales problem. People attach emotion and expectation to joining your association. Will my competition be there? Will people be friendly? Will I have something to contribute?

One of the most profound realizations I've ever had came from a speaker at the Canadian Chamber of Commerce Annual General Meeting of 2010, the Vice President & Head of Strategy for Sid Lee, a Montreal-based creative services firm.

*"If you don't tell your story,
the public will make up
one about you."*
*~ Eric Alper*

I've been teaching branding strategies to businesses and non-profits for a decade, but that simple statement almost eliminates the need for lessons: *If you don't tell your story, they will make up one about you.*

The instruction behind the statement is shockingly simple: Tell your story.

It's not, "Keep advertising on price and tell a story," or, "Come up with a clever slogan and a story." Just *tell your story.*

I find that most membership organizations don't tell their story very well. Scratch that: I find that *most organizations* don't tell their story well, regardless of business model or tax status.

When the message is clear, the money comes easy. If you are a business-focused membership organization, are your members not your product? If members benefit from your services, do they not become your story?

Perhaps your story is better told by your members.

# The Pain Funnel

Sandler Sales Institute helped to reverse my bad sales habits early on. I didn't realize I suffered from these habits until one day in 2003 when I received a membership returned renewal invoice. On it was written a note: "Not renewing this year. No time to participate."

Even though I hadn't sold that member, I took it personally. I was so tired of people telling us they didn't have time to participate. Didn't they realize that we are so much more than events? No, because we had only been reporting to them about events.

The photos in your newsletter are of people at your events. Headlines covering past events might read, "See what you've been missing." Videos showing how much fun your members have at your events contribute to the unintended consequence of having great events.

The unintended consequence is that you reward members who show up at the expense of those who don't.

'No time to participate'
isn't just a reason to
cancel a membership;
it's an escape from
the guilt and punishment
you've been issuing as your
members focus on other
priorities.

Sandler Sales Institute's Paula Creekmore of Eugene, Oregon, says the way to engage a member is to solve their problems. Simple enough, right?

The pain funnel refers to a series of questions used to discover the problems you can solve for your member or prospect. In my experience, this method results in lasting memberships and partnerships rather than participants.

Just like a consultant, go into a membership meeting with a business card and a pad of paper, ready to take notes. There is no "membership packet," no information dump, and no folder full of flyers, programs or menus.

Just ask the business owner what their top three pains are.

Pains? Yes, pains. Ask them what about their business keeps them up at night.

Usually, item one is something revenue-related: competition, sales, advertising, marketing and branding. Item two is usually cost-related: taxes, employment costs, human resources management, or the rising costs of fuel and supplies. Item three is usually something specific to their industry.

If you're an industry-specific association, you can most likely respond to all three pains. For chambers of commerce, you can help with numbers one and two only.

You've written their top three pains down on your paper without allowing them to go into too much detail at this point. Now, turn your paper back to them and tell them you can help them with numbers one or two. "Which would you like to talk about?"

Whichever they choose, you're bringing them into your pain funnel by asking them to tell you more about the issue. Then, this series:

> "What have you tried?"
> "How long did it take?"
> "How much did it cost?"
> "Did it work? Yes or no..."

Then, "What else did you try? How long did it take? How much did it cost? Did it work? Yes or no..." And again, and again, and again, until the prospect runs out of answers.

You add up the time and money so you can report back to them the resources they have thrown at the problem. "Are you ready to try something else?" I've never met someone who declined at this point.

These new sales habits will keep you from being put into the box entitled *sales person.*

## Pulling the Deal off the Table

A friend of mine once shared with me a comment from a therapist: "You teach people how to treat you." This has helped me to better manage relationships and professional situations alike.

When you're expected to behave as a salesperson, but you don't, you stand out. One example happened in 2003 when I met with a member to talk about renewing an advertising agreement.

The member was evading the purpose of the meeting, so rather than redirect the conversation as other sales people would, I put away my advertising samples and last year's tear sheets, and took out my pad of paper to take notes.

After exhausting his off topic conversation to the point he had shared it all, I explained that I would take his comments back to our staff so that his perspective was known on the topics he cares about, and that I was sorry he's not ready to consider advertising.

He was shocked. As I packed up my things, he stopped me in my tracks, and returned with the checkbook.

Prospects get defensive and often feel like prey. Applicants will explain why they qualify for what you offer. The chasm between these two strategies is vast, much like the difference between a two-year member and a lifetime member.

## The List

The Florida Chamber of Commerce goes in with a business card and a list. They talk about their purpose, exclusively. "It's going to take four million dollars to fight sue-happy lawyers, rising workers' compensation insurance rates and a growing anti-business sentiment in our state," they pitch. "How much are you in for? This list contains the companies that have committed $20,000 a year or more."

Most businesses, if they are committed to your cause, will first take note of who is on the list. Then they will notice who is missing from it. There is a certain amount of influence that goes along with this sort of subtlety.

## Ought-to, Want-to, Have-to

If you've ever conducted a cattle call for your association in the form of a membership drive, you've probably also noticed that your association loses a greater percentage of new members from membership drives than from other times of the year.

This is because your organization didn't adjust your member orientation, training and acclimation processes accordingly.

Keith Woods, CEO of the North Coast Builders Exchange and former CEO of the Santa Rosa (CA) Chamber of Commerce, is a popular speaker and trainer for associations for decades. Woods says there are three types of members:

- The Have-to's,
- The Ought-to's, and
- The Want-to's

When you run a membership drive, or your incoming board president calls on someone to join your association, they are creating Have-to's in your organization. You got their money. Fine.

But play this out with me. Someone walks into the Have-to's business and says, "I see from the plaque on the wall that you're a member of the chamber of commerce."

The Have-to shrugs her shoulders, rolls her eyes a little, and says, "I had to." This is a drag on your brand.

The Ought-to joined long ago. They get what you do and why you do it. They appreciate your organization, even though they admit they aren't familiar with the depth of your function. They renew quietly each year. Depending on the age of your organization, we need these members.

Side note: I believe Ought-to's aren't out there anymore as membership prospects for most associations, especially chambers of commerce.

I call these "Legacy Businesses." They are deeply entrenched in their network or industry. They don't pay any mind to social media trends, and might still have their first website from 1999. They are more interested in sun-setting than reinventing. They may be a professional services firm or manufacturing conglomerate. Perhaps they still advertise in the yellow pages, but it's just to reassure people that they are still in business.

The Want-to is your ideal member, and the future of your membership development efforts. She is actively seeking solutions to her business challenges.

But you've been scaring away Want-to's for years. You haven't trained them on the pathways to follow in order to achieve their business goals. You've used voodoo codes and secret handshakes to create a rumor mill around how to do business with you.

**The lost opportunity for revenue with this crowd pales in comparison to the lost opportunity for engagement. These are the active members who want to love you if you'll just let them.**

Be easy to work with. Have pricing and packaging that reflects your strength and flexibility. Be open to their involvement from the get-go, without a waiting period. Connect them to their peers within your membership and reassure them right away that they are in the right place.

You teach people how to treat you. You also teach people with whom you want to do business. Nurturing the Want-to member will attract more of the same. Numerous organizations go cold-calling door-to-door instead of asking their bread-and-butter members a simple question: "What can we do to be more valuable to you?"

Building a better mousetrap means designing your systems around the member instead of around your staff or internal protocol.

## Membership Dues Models

### Fair Share Dues

Fair share dues structures are based on the number of employees, the value of assets, or the annual revenues of a business. These scaled amounts match to a schedule of dues to determine how much a business pays to be a member of an association or a chamber of commerce.

> 1-5 Employees: $250
> 6-10 Employees: $300
> 11-15 Employees: $350
> 16-25 Employees: $450
> 26-50 Employees: $700
> 51-75 Employees: $950
> 76-100 Employees: $1,200
> 100+ Employees: $25 each 5

This is not the ideal pricing model for tomorrow's membership organization for a number of reasons.

- Benefits are the same regardless of investment
- Does not segment or differentiate members
- A la carte purchasing requires multiple "asks"
- Punishes businesses for growing

**Investor Levels**

> Chairman's Circle: $2,500
> Platinum Club: $5,000

Investor levels, sometimes called Chairman's Circles, President's Clubs, Platinum Roundtables, etc, are a pay-to-play program which may function as an additional membership with a specific set of benefits.

- Flat rate fee
- Specific benefit
- Funds sometimes dedicated to cause or program

**Membership Tiers**

Membership tiers are packages of benefits which entice larger investments in dues organizations.

Business Tier: $350
Preferred Tier: $625
Premium Tier: $1,250
Executive Tier: $2,500
President's Tier: $5,000

Tiers are also known to use a Mission Appeal and/or a Recognition Appeal to attract buyers to a higher level of investment.

- Based on choice
- Benefits increase with investment
- Grows with business-member
- Segments and differentiates members
- Simplified annual planning and purchasing
- Specific reason for buying

# Tiers, Not Tears

As someone who coaches chambers of commerce through the conversion from the (un)fair-share model to the tiered model, I repeatedly get asked the same questions about tiers. Here they are for your consideration.

**We're concerned that too many of our members are too small for tiers.**

Tiers work because of small business, not in spite of them. Now your smallest members can play with the big boys and girls. Business owners have needs, egos, and expectations. Allowing them to buy at a level that matches their preference is capitalism at its finest.

**Can an organization be too small for tiers?**

I don't believe so. This model transcends size, scope or territory.

**Why would we switch to tiers?**

Well for one, if you use a fair-share model now, you are punishing your members for growing, and rewarding them for lying to you. Neither of these are a good premise for a long-lasting relationship. Plus, your members are already doing business this way, just not with your organization. Fast food restaurants, cable and satellite television companies, health clubs... They all use tiered packaging in some way. This isn't new; it's just new to associations.

## How do we prevent large investors from reducing their investment?

First, build an incredible tier package that rewards a higher level of monetary investment. Then use what I call the "reverse-employee-count safety net" whereby large employers are not eligible for lower membership. This is a great transition from fair-share models. The key here is to put this in the fine print so that it is not the starting point, but just a safety net. Hence the name.

## Do tiers still feature a fair-share component?

They certainly could, but I don't believe they should. It is important to get buy-in from your members in free market fashion. The safety net is used in a purchase transaction, not in the needs analysis and selection process.

## Can tiers be customized?

Yes. From associations to chambers of commerce, no two tiered membership plans are the same. (If there are, you haven't considered the uniqueness of your membership.) Members should be encouraged to customize their membership. In sales terms, this is called *up-selling*.

Most packages are a starting point from which we create a customized plan for servicing a member or client. *"I'll have a number two super-sized with a Coke."* Through some very simple marketing and sales techniques, your marketing materials can reflect the customizable nature of tiers, encouraging members to make each package their own.

**Where do we begin?**

First, make a list of all the benefits you offer members for their dues.

Second, add on the features of your chamber for which you charge members. This includes business services, advertising tickets and ticket packages, subscriptions, programs, trainings, et cetera. (Don't include event sponsorships for this exercise.) Put an X next to any of these items which are limited in supply, or sell out. We're not going to use these just yet.

Third, quantify the value of each feature using a reasonable conversion rate and average sale. (See *Quantify Your Un-Quantified Values* on page 55.) Start moving these benefits into packages with your members in mind, and you're well on your way.

## How do we get our board on-board?

Remember that your board consists of members. They want more value, too. Tiers will do two things for you: raise revenue, and increase value. Which are they more resistant to? Price increases. Focus on how tiers will improve the value for members. Many organizations have gone the other way, causing the proposal to be rejected by the board. If you can't get your board excited about this idea, it is because you have focused on what's easy. Raising the value is hard.

## Should we be selling from low-to-high or high-to-low?

I learned this lesson the hard way when I realized I was selling the high-priced membership tier from the back of the brochure to a member who was a legitimate prospect for the highest tier. Big spenders prefer to buy from the front of the catalog, not the back.

There is a reason grocery stores put the milk in the back of the store; it's so you have to walk through the other stuff to get there, tempted along the way there, and on the way back. Simple staple item: milk. It's just like simple staple item: basic membership. To get there, we're going to tempt you along the way.

So, sell high-to-low. Make the prospect see and consider all of the things that they will be passing up by selecting a lower tier. At the very least, they will have a better understanding of what it is that your organization actually does.

## How do we track the delivery of benefits?

The problem, as I see it, is that your organization may have not been accountable for service delivery. You could use vouchers or a coupon book as a delivery and tracking mechanism, but by themselves, they do not have a personal service component desired by higher investors.

In all my research, I haven't found any reproducible system for tracking, so I created one. My clients have access to the tools and video training to get your entire staff involved in tracking these items, because it's your entire staff that is delivering them.

It's a simple system, really, but most associations would prefer to automate this process. If your database or customer relationship management (CRM) system allows you to cluster benefits while tracking them independently, then you have the capability to automate the tracking.

## Should we upgrade members throughout the year, or upon renewal?

Both are needed for a successful result from your conversion to tiers. If you're on an anniversary renewal program, pull out members you'd like to visit about two or three months prior to their renewal date and hand-deliver the renewal invoice with the new tier options listed... but only the higher tiers should be displayed. They've demonstrated that you're worth what they have been investing, so don't give them the option to downgrade their investment unless the other option is losing them as a member.

## What will tiers do for sales and retention?

Converting to tiers is not a solution to your sales or retention problem. However, some associations report higher new member revenue due to a choice instead of yes-or-no pitch.

Most organizations see a higher dues-per-member average. At the Salem Area Chamber of Commerce, average annual dues were up 25 percent after less than two years, and new member revenue was up nearly 20 percent after just one year.

One of the subtleties of a successful tiered dues plan is in the pricing. After researching my own membership drops, I found that retention increased dramatically for those members investing more than $500 per year. It's no accident that next membership level was priced above this threshold at $650. This move allows an organization to focus retention efforts in accordance with our priorities.

You might think it's obvious to focus your retention efforts on those members investing less than $500 per year, but simple math suggests that, given Member A is investing $325 and Member B is investing $650, your efforts to retain Member B will yield twice the results for the same effort.

## What would we do with our Chairman's Circle program?

Many business-focused membership organizations have a premium membership such as a Chairman's Circle, or Trustees Membership. In most cases, this level can be easily blended into your new tiers. For example, it could become your highest or second-highest tier, depending on the number of members, price, value and market.

## How do we assign a dollar value to tiers?

Use formulas used by media ad buyers and IEG for accuracy, and then pair that with conservative numbers of impressions for realistic values you can take to the bank. The quantification worksheets mentioned earlier in this book will be of great help. Get them online at RemembershipBook.com.

**Our staff and board members are concerned about taking away benefits that members have been receiving for years.**

I don't endorse taking away any benefits. Your current benefits will be your basic business tier. This obviously puts pressure on your organization to add benefits to complete your marketable packages. That's where a consultant like me comes in. You and your staff may not have the time or experience to do the necessary research I've acquired since 2004.

**Will members who don't upgrade feel less important?**

The point here is to put a higher value on your de-valued organization. Price is an important component of value. The question, therefore, really is, "Why do you let these businesses de-value your organization by investing less than it costs to serve them?"

By investing at the minimum level, below your cost-per-member benchmark, are they not telling you that they should be less important to you? That they aren't committed to your cause? That they won't be around long enough for you to take notice?

REMEMBER: Find your cost-per-member benchmark. This is what it costs you to do what you do for each member annually. Total revenue minus any grants or government contracts divided by the number of members equals your cost-per-member. (Some experts recommend removing all program revenue, as well. I leave it in under the assumption that your programs fit your mission and function.)

Don't think for a moment that I'm casting aside the membership model. The default business plan of a membership organization requires that many paying members offset the costs incurred by the high-needs members.

This does not take into account the power of choice. When given a choice, a portion of your membership will choose a higher level. If you price your tiers correctly for your organization and market, this portion of members can bring an increase in revenue.

When I was in the health club business, we had great concern that two members, side by side on a treadmill, would get to talking about how much they each paid in membership dues. If one had a corporate rate, the other might feel like their membership at the club wasn't worth what they were paying. That type of pricing is often mistakenly called "promotional pricing." It should be called "de-motional pricing." Lowering prices, couponing and discounting is not a promotion if it lowers your value in the eyes of the consumer.

Put a new price on the worth of your association by creating clear levels of service. One effect of having these tiers is that when someone feels they aren't getting the right level of service or benefits, the solution is as simple as putting them in the right membership.

**Tiers Round Up**

Make no mistake: this is a new way of thinking for your old-school membership organization. Adding a premium price for status hasn't been talked about since "Chairman's Circles" in associations. This is the first step. Now build the rest of the rungs for the ladder that can take any business from the bottom to the top.

My answers to these questions may seem harsh at times, but I have the benefit of learning by doing. Through the conversion process, I was the graphic designer who designed the award-winning marketing materials, the salesman who tested the packages, the researcher who sought out the best and worst in my industry, and the marketer who planned and executed the launch and collateral. Since then, I've done the same thing for numerous other membership organizations.

## Membership Drive Intervention

Years ago, I wrote an open letter to chambers of commerce who were burning through volunteers and churning through members with membership drives. I seriously doubt that I was the first to talk about it, but I still run into people who tell me they pass this around to staff and board members. I hear it's even posted in association break-rooms.

*Dear Chamber of Commerce,*

*It's because I love you that I write this letter. Please give up membership drives. I understand how a chamber could get addicted to membership-driving, so I'm not judging you. When your chamber needs that kick, and your budget counts on it, the rush of members going through your system can feel so great!*

*But the lows are low. When you need another hit of members and you've already smoked them all, where do you go? Another membership drive? Do you call your doctor and get the patch?*

Quitting cold-turkey seems a daunting task. If you don't find something else soon, you're going to start drinking again and it's a downward spiral from there.

So now you're up to two drives a year to feed your habit. Members stop referring year-round because they are waiting for a drive. Those referrals were like endorphins to your nervous system. Now there are basically two times per year that you get to feel the high of new members running through your system.

Your addiction to new members will eventually cause your volunteers to organize an intervention. "We're tired of calling on businesses twice a year," they say. "And we feel like we don't even know you anymore." A wedge has been driven between you.

"We just want our membership director back," they plea. "The one we loved before all of the membership-driving began." They're hoping you won't turn to violence... or worse, a fundraising consultant.

Let's not even get into all of the enablers... The codependency runs deep into your board and CEO. They look the other way in order to have the dollars in the bank, and they aren't helping a bit. Your treasurer will not show up for the intervention.

What if you could replace the nicotine of membership drives with the endorphins of an ongoing referral *system? It would be like replacing smoking with jogging. The benefits to the health of your organization would be tremendous.*

*Imagine, no more massive exodus from your membership upon the first year anniversary. No more calling on a prospect only to be turned away with, "I tried it a few years ago and I didn't get any service, so I dropped it."*

*What if you were to bring on new members at a pace that could gain you a better relationship with them, instead of just a turn-and-burn? I bet you'd get more dollars per member per year. I bet your average length of membership would increase over time. And I bet you'd be perceived as an engaging organization that's doing great things without the cloud of a pressured referral-sales organization.*

*Quitting Membership Drives Now Greatly Reduces Serious Risks to Your Chamber's Health.*

There is one condition under which I would endorse your organization conduct a membership drive, and it is only when you have a system for serving masses of members. Even then, few markets can endure annual – or even bi-annual – campaigns. I don't think we need to talk about membership drives anymore in this book.

# Quantify Your Un-Quantified Values

Mike Varney was the founder and CEO of Symphony Marketing in Wisconsin before moving to Las Vegas to head-up the marketing department of the Las Vegas Chamber of Commerce. As this book goes to print, Mike has just accepted a new role as CEO of the chamber of commerce in Tucson, Arizona.

I met Mike four years into his innovations at the Las Vegas Chamber, but this story starts in Wisconsin. Symphony Marketing was a small marketing and sales firm conceived after spending two decades as a broadcast executive.

Twenty-six years of media experience collided with a membership organization in April of 1997. The result was a simple worksheet Mike and his team created to convert every single benefit of membership in the Las Vegas Chamber into a quantified value which contributes to the return on the member's investment.

Members of the chamber get a single listing in thousands of directories printed annually. How much is that worth? Have you ever thought about it? What else do we know about the directory?

Let's just say...

- 2,000 directories printed
- An average directory is referenced five times per year for a buying decision
- 1,000 members in the directory
- A third of these shoppers will buy
- An average purchase is $35 (A coffee drink is $3.50, a new car is $35,000... $35 is reasonable and conservative)
- 2000 x 5 / 1000 / 3 x $35 = $116

A listing in your association's directory is worth $116. This exercise can be done with every benefit of your membership.

 REMEMBER: Download a worksheet at RemembershipBook.com to help you turn your memberships into quantified values.

## Qualify Your Unqualified Prospects

John Bosse is the Vice President of Small Business for The Cincinnati USA Regional Chamber. I asked John, a veteran of almost fourteen years for his membership organization, about how he determines who is a good prospect for his chamber.

"We look for companies with ten employees or more," he explained. John has figured out that, while they will sign up any business that comes to them, their bread-and-butter business members have ten or more employees. They are stable. They have specific, definable needs which his membership organization can fulfill. As a result, the Cincinnati USA Regional Chamber has a higher retention rate than most other chambers of commerce its size.

 REMEMBER: Look at your canceled memberships. Go into records for the last three to five years to find the zip codes, employee counts, dues amounts, membership longevity and total purchases. If you filter your data for any of these features, you'll find some valuable information.

If you charge for dues based on employee-count, then you won't be able to filter the dues data. Your members don't have a choice in their dues. You could still use the total investment as criteria, but subtracting the non-optional dues amount will be a more accurate filter.

After performing the exercise above, we can look at Cincinnati's revelation and realize that it wasn't just the dollar amount contributing to the increase (although we can still make that argument), it was the employee count.

How do you qualify your members? And how do you assess their dues? Are they related?

John Bosse's simple acknowledgment of his most qualified member allows him to focus his service and retention efforts on businesses which will make the most impact to the organization.

REMEMBER: Study your membership to discover how many members have 10 or more employees, and how many have fewer. Look for other ways to group your membership, depending on your specific organization. Evaluate the retention rate of each group, even by first year, second, third and beyond. Admit that you may be better with one kind of member over another, then prospect for the preferred business profile, and shore up your weaknesses. Make strategic changes to improve the satisfaction of these members who are most likely to churn, or get rid of them altogether.

If you know your association has just a 50 percent retention rate of first year members, imagine what you can do to your retention rate if you can increase first year renewals by just 5-10 percent.

## Satisfaction Does Not Make Loyalty

It's truly a confusing time when we receive cancellation notices reading, "You've done a terrific job, and I'm not dissatisfied in any way, but I won't be renewing my membership this year."

It's tempting to skirt the issue by removing annual renewals for your organization. Switching to invisible, low, automatic monthly payments seems a brilliant idea.

*Health clubs have been doing business this way since the 80s*, you think to yourself. IHRSA, the International Health, Racquet and Sportsclub Association, reports health clubs have an average retention rate of 75 percent. If this rate was higher, I would support this argument, but most associations have retention rates higher than this.

So we're left to grapple with this issue of member loyalty without regard to trickery or invisible payment mechanisms.

Business blogger and marketing game-changer Seth Godin says we must turn strangers into friends, friends into customers, and customers into loyal customers. Godin is the author of *Linchpin, Tribes, The Dip*, and *Purple Cow* to name just a few of his 12 best-sellers. This particular directive comes from his 1999 book *Permission Marketing*.

I recently re-read *Permission Marketing* to see if his prediction of the future of marketing was still on point, given the social media movement in full force as I write this. In 1999, the burning issue Godin was addressing was specific to email and website marketing. Godin is brilliant, and *Permission Marketing* is still important. I suspect that is why he has never re-written it.

When you visit a web site and they ask you to enter your name and email address to access specific information or receive an electronic newsletter, this is permission marketing. You are giving the publisher permission to market to you.

Social media is similar. When someone "likes" your business on Facebook or follows you on Twitter, they are giving you permission to market to them. It is a different kind of marketing they want, however.

The top 10 reasons consumers follow a company, according to research reported by *Social Media Today*:

- 40% want to receive discounts and promotions
- 37% want to show support for the brand/company to others
- 36% want get free samples or coupons
- 34% want to stay informed about the activities of the company
- 33% want to get updates on future products
- 30% want to get updates and information on future sales
- 27% like to get fun and entertainment out of it
- 25% want to get access to exclusive content

- 22% mentioned they were referred by someone to follow this brand/company
- 21% want just to learn more about the company

The purpose of permission is to turn strangers into friends. This is the first critical conversion. Based on the top 10 reasons consumers follow you on social media, calling them "fans" would be a stretch.

True loyalty is internal, not external. I don't think that, just because your wireless company makes it difficult to switch to another carrier, this can be interpreted as loyalty. Similarly, your health club's two-year agreement and relatively quiet deduction of their dues from your bank account cannot be interpreted as loyalty.

Another note on Godin: You could read *Tribes* and replace the word "tribe" with the name of your association in almost every instance. Read it, and then read it again because he makes some points more elegant than simple.

*"Loyalty is what we call it when someone refuses a momentarily better option."*

*~ Seth Godin*

# What was the Question?

Put associations from different regions and markets in a room and the questions begin: How many members do you have? What is your retention rate? Is that in dollars or number of members? What is your turnover? What is your conversion rate?

Stephanie Kirksey says if you want new answers, ask new questions. Kirksey is the executive vice president for the Greater Richmond (VA) Chamber, and a co-conspirator in my quest to change membership development strategies among membership organizations.

In a newsletter column as chair of the membership development division of the American Chamber of Commerce Executives, she suggests we ask questions like: *Who are our members? Do we have the "right" members? Are our members engaged? Are we spending all of our time on the members that offer the least or the most financial opportunity to the organization? Do the bigger/key companies find clear value in the chamber? Do members know how to optimize their membership?*

*"Change the questions and you might change the answers."*
*~Stephanie Kirksey*

# Have More Bad Ideas

Many associations are lemurs. Most chambers of commerce certainly are, as well. They follow the leader. They copy the map of any program with results, regardless of the relative impact on their own customer base.

This is fine by itself, but I fear the message it sends is one of complacency. Rather than ask your members how you can help them, you have relied on one of your counterparts to ask their members the question, devise an answer, and hope they share the results with you.

The risk is that you'll be perceived as too safe. Put a different way, if you want to be known as a resource where your members can find solutions, then solve something. Take a risk. Fail at something new. At least you tried something new, and hopefully it was something designed to solve a problem your members actually have.

I've failed with plenty of new offerings to my membership base. There are two noteworthy points about failures: One, members don't remember your failures, and two, you learn something from each failure that makes you a more valuable organization.

To have more good ideas, start generating more bad ideas. If it's a numbers game, the good ones are in there. The challenge is in knowing the difference; that is the "art," as Godin explains in *Linchpin*.

## Expectations Have Changed

Perhaps the best reason for the existence of this book is that the nature of your membership organization hasn't kept up with consumer expectations. The proliferation of social networks, online banking, paperless statements, and a Wikipedia world has transformed behaviors and forever set new expectations for your organization.

It's not hard to find reasons to satisfy these expectations. They lead to greater revenue, deeper customer knowledge, better efficiency and leaner organizations.

Social networks have lowered the cost of connecting people (to zero). High were the barriers that used to be in place to get an introduction to a potential future customer or vendor. Join an organization and pay their dues, wear your business clothes to a networking event and start working the pond. (Tip of the hat to Darcy Rezac, Gayle Rezac and Judy Thompson, authors of *Work the Pond*, a great book about how, why and where to build relationships.)

Thanks to Facebook, LinkedIn, and thousands of other social networks, you don't have to join anything, pay anything, or even get dressed in the morning to find prospects and potential partners.

What these technologies don't do, however, is instigate relationships. If you're concerned that social networks are encroaching on your space, remember that you can create a culture which not only encourages relationships, but instigates them, too. Your culture can't necessarily be re-created on the Internet. If it can, that's a different problem.

It's important to note that an online world benefits the lazy and socially unskilled. If someone wants only to take from the pool, maybe it is better that they do so online instead of within your organization.

These sharks will scare away the big fish. More than ever before, your members value peer-to-peer connections. If you ignore this fact, don't be surprised when your connection events are over-run by salespeople, each of them trying to sell the other.

When you chase new revenue by lowering your price point, offering monthly memberships, and short-term trials, you are inviting this potentially negative element into your membership organization. I think it is fine to explore these options, but do so with that critical truth in mind.

Never betray your crew by inviting the pirates aboard your ship.

## Build a Better Mousetrap

Conversations regarding how financial institutions engage with their customers contain clues for membership organizations to follow.

In their book *Made to Stick*, authors Chip Heath and Dan Heath explore what makes ideas last while others die. They share a story of an un-named bank in the process of evaluating whether to invest more in online services for their customers. At the time, 10 percent of their customers logged in to their accounts through the bank's web site.

At first glance, this isn't setting up a good argument to invest more for existing customers, so it's a good thing they dug deeper to find out who these customers were.

The bank discovered that this small sector of their customer base represented 70 percent of monthly deposits. This singular finding was pure gold for their business plan.

By identifying this common thread among their ideal customer, the bank could build a better mousetrap to attract more of the same.

## The Referral Age has Replaced the Information Age

Information is no longer a membership benefit. The proliferation of stats and facts is not exclusive to your organization. It's out there, somewhere.

In a time when search engines correct your spelling and intuitively suggest other search terms to provide more accurate results, it's safe to say that information is everywhere, and people don't care where it comes from.

People would rather take the recommendation of a complete stranger than conduct their own due diligence based on available information.

Because of this, the most effective communications strategies include creating your own content and adding a filter, or perspective, to other current news and information.

*Advertising Age* does a terrific job of this. Think about their audience. Folks who are successful in the business of creating advertisements for an increasingly attention-deprived world are probably a little A.D.D. themselves. *Advertising Age* has to be good at what they do.

By the time I receive my *Advertising Age* magazine in the mail, I've seen most of the articles from my email subscriptions. They have divided up their entire magazine into different interest areas and sent them out electronically in a more timely fashion.

But we don't mind a bit. We have a different expectation of digital communications. They must be timely if they are to be relevant.

Your membership organization likely has a print newsletter and (various) emails. Your newsletter may already contain the makings of several e-publications for segmented audiences amongst your membership.

An aside on electronic communications: If you suspect you are sending out too many emails to your membership, you probably are. If you wonder about the open-rates of your emails, you'll be appalled at how few are being read.

If you haven't been enforcing a policy for your staff about the frequency of sending emails -- or you don't have one -- you may have already lost the opportunity to communicate with your membership by email.

Fix it now. No more than one email a week. Start with the Rule of 6s and evolve from there: No more than six items per email, no more than six lines per item, and no more than six words per headline. If you can't say it in six lines, include a link to your web site.

Keep it concise. Never repeat the same article from a previous week. Resist the urge to send out a mass email for a special purpose which provides value only to you. Use targeted or special interest lists for this, instead.

Segmenting your communications seems like a daunting task, but your relevance depends on it. It could be that, by subjecting your members to content in which they are not interested, you've turned them off already.

If a member has told you (in words or actions) they are not interested in attending events, the event-heavy promotional messages in your electronic communications may as well read, "We don't want you as a member if you don't come to our events."

## Communicating in an Advertising Age

How would *Advertising Age* overhaul your communications? Let's say your print newsletter contains:

- A Feature story
- Your upcoming events
- Column from the CEO
- Industry or advocacy update
- Column from the board chair
- News from members
- Events from members
- Timely stats & trends

Segment 1: *Insights* contains the columns from your CEO and board chair, plus timely stats and trends

Segment 2: *E-vents* features your events, plus upcoming events submitted by members

Segment 3: *Newsroom* includes news items (not events) submitted by members

Segment 4: *Insider* would include only the industry or advocacy work of your organization.

If you've been keeping track, the only part of your print newsletter not included in your new email segments is the cover story, which provides value to those who want to spend time with your printed publication.

The hard part will be allowing members to pick and choose which e-publications they want without your interference. Perhaps the hardest part will be sending out these e-pubs before your print newsletter hits mailboxes.

Forcing publications on members is a disservice, not a membership benefit.

*Tomorrow's membership organization has the confidence to let the member choose—and control—the information they want to receive from you.*

# The Safety of Being Mediocre

It used to be that consumers were content to do business however the business wanted it. That's fine if you're a wireless company where difficult is the norm for the whole industry.

Over the last decade, the banking industry has been waking up to the marketing power of transparency and customization. This is driven largely by competition.

In the association world, your domain is being encroached in nearly every way. Alternatives exist for every feature of membership. *I can replace your marketing benefits with advertising or SEO, no problem. Your chamber of commerce advocacy won't be missed if I use a combination of lobbyists, attorneys and industry-specific associations.*

As a group, membership organizations are bland. As Seth Godin points out in *Poke the Box*, "You can't get blander than bland."

Could it be that you have set the bar at mediocre? "We almost never look at merely mediocre products and wonder why they aren't great," writes Godin. "Mediocre services or products do what they're supposed to, but have set the bar so low that it's hardly worth the energy to cross the street to buy them."

Therein lies the problem you face. Unremarkable services from mediocre organizations don't attract fans. When was the last time someone said to you, "You really have to try this vanilla ice cream"? Vanilla is taken. It's been done.

Your vanilla dues model is indefensible. The resulting confusion has infected the rest of the organization, staff included. I remember making up a reason for why my chamber charged dues based on the number of employees: "The impact of our advocacy is greater for larger employers."

But advocacy isn't bought; it's sold. Education and information products and insurance are the same way. The industry must make the case for its relevance by telling their story.

I know exactly what I want from my wireless company and government: I want them to be a relatively invisible utility.

I know exactly what I want from my insurance company: defend me and protect me if something bad happens.

I know exactly what I want from my car: fire up when I put in the key.

Ask any member what they want from your organization and they likely won't know how to answer you. Perhaps this has changed over time. Maybe people used to know what they wanted from you.

Perhaps there just isn't a schema for your association. If there isn't an expectation, it's all too easy to make only the simplest of improvements.

If your organization is a twig in a river's current representing the movement of society, you are flowing along just fine. According to Godin, if you are a rock tumbling along the bottom, you are never going to keep up with the current.

## What Ever Happened to the Original Social Network?

Joe Abraham, known as the Entrepreneur's biggest fan, writes blogs about chambers of commerce in a persistently challenging tone.

"It used to be that I could join a chamber, and it would impact my business," Joe writes. "I would have access to proven education that I could implement in my business. I could meet other business owners and be encouraged through the ups and downs of business. I would have such a positive experience both personally and financially, that I would have no choice but to tell every business owner I know about the chamber.

"Question: Are there any fanatical customers left in your chamber of commerce?"

Most associations have a similar challenge ahead of them. With so much competition and online "noise" competing for the same audience, you have a hundred sources where there once were very few.

## You Don't Function in Isolation

Chambers of commerce will qualify their ability to benchmark against each other by whether or not the organization acts as the convention and visitors' bureau, or economic development arm of the city?

Who cares? Turf is a nasty thing. It is usually paired with ego and politics. If you are a chamber of commerce, you produce what the economic development organization sells. And even if someone else serves as your community's convention and visitors' bureau (CVB), your organization produces what the CVB sells.

Maura Gast, executive director of the Irving Texas Convention & Visitors Bureau puts this into perfect perspective:

*"If you build a place where people want to visit, you build a place where people want to live. If you build a place where people want to live, you build a place where people want to work. If you build a place where people want to work, you build a place where business needs to be. And if you build a place where business has to be, you'll build a place where people have to visit."*

Once you figure out where you are in this cycle of function, you'll realize that the more you respect each other's turf, the worse job you are doing.

In a visit to Santa Rosa, California, I was invited to dinner at John Ash & Co, a legendary restaurant located at the beautiful Vintner's Inn. That night, they had two menus. The second menu was part of a county-wide promotion called Restaurant Week. More than 100 restaurants across Sonoma County offer a three-course menu for $19, $29, or $39.

Turns out, it's not the Santa Rosa CVB or Chamber of Commerce that run this promotion; it's the Sonoma County Economic Development Board. To me, this is a sign that Sonoma County has starters in the right places. I know of a thousand regions where Restaurant Week would have been sabotaged or resented because it encroaches on someone else's turf. That's just not right.

Gast's comment forces you to consider the partners involved in your endeavor. For chambers, CVBs and EDCs, the relationship is pretty clear: to foster or create competition among regional organizations is to undermine the relationship.

Instead of getting permission, start something. It sure would be nice to break out of this "turf" thing. Create a culture of innovation in your region, industry or organization by granting permission to start things. Innovate.

## Pro-Active Renewals

The West Virginia Chamber of Commerce works on renewals the hard way. They pick up the phone to touch base with each member, eventually asking permission to mail a renewal invoice for another year of membership.

It should come as no surprise that Amanda Pasdon, their director of business investment and development, spent a lot of time at the podium of a conference where awards for innovative membership development practices were honored. The West Virginia Chamber of Commerce cleaned up.

Pasdon and President Steve Roberts have figured out that great pro-active customer service yields positive changes in member retention.

## On Buying and Justifying

People buy emotionally and they justify intellectually. For membership organizations, people join emotionally and they justify upon renewal. This means you have a year to help them justify their investment in your organization.

Connected members are engaged in your organization because you've captured their heart. If you haven't connected with a member in the first year of their membership, you'll likely lose them for good. According to statements from business people interviewed about their membership experiences for this book, some are willing to give you a second year, but not a third.

If members are dropping because of the improper way you've sold the membership in the first place, then replacing a dropped member with a new one, or even two new ones, isn't going to solve your membership problem.

Consider which members stay for the long-term. Go get more of those. If you can't find them, ask your long-term members where they might be.

## To Whom are You Referring?

The Greater Omaha Chamber of Commerce developed a referral program which allows loyal members to receive a nice perk when their friends and business associates join. Vice President of Small Business and Membership Jim Butler applies a full 10 percent of the new member's dues to the referring member's next renewal. When Jim called me for my thoughts on his idea, I told him he was crazy, and that I was crazy enough to steal the idea.

I get a lot of these calls from Jim Butler. I suspect it's because he cut his business development teeth outside of the chamber industry. It's a good thing Jim isn't doing what chambers are "supposed to." He probably doesn't eat vanilla ice cream, either. This isn't a new concept, but I had never seen a chamber of commerce pull this off.

When I started my first business in 1994, I bought a pager. (Remember those?) The paging company would put perforated sheets of business-card-sized referral cards, three or more, in my monthly statements. To refer someone to them, I just handed one of their cards with my pager number written on it to someone. When they brought it in to sign up, we both received a free month of service. I didn't pay for paging service after the first month because of this.

AudioAcrobat.com has a similarly aggressive growth strategy. They take the paging company's program a step further.

AudioAcrobat is an online host for audio recordings. I use it to play radio interviews, podcasts, and the like.

Their best feature, in my opinion, is the ability to make a recording for online use from your telephone. After you record or upload your audio files, you select a player and embed it on your website.

When you opt in for their referral program, each of your players is coded with a referral code specific to your account. Someone will play audio on your site and say, "Hey what is this cool little audio player thing?" When they click on the player, the user is taken to a tour of their service. When they join, the referring user receives 33 percent of the new user's fees for the lifetime of each subscription.

Signing up to be a referral partner is easy. You just have to click a button.

If your membership organization can find a way to implement this type of referral program, you win. (Coincidentally, if you sign up for AudioAcrobat at http://kylethink.audioacrobat.com, I win, too.)

## Stories: Humanity in Your Brand

Tom's Shoes puts great stories of charity into a box of shoes and mails them to you for money. Go to Toms.com and see for yourself.

Burt's Bees sells saving the earth, and my favorite lip balm. It's too bad membership organizations don't produce anything. Or do they?

Your members' joyful loyalty is your product. The unique attributes of your members' stories becomes your story. Their fears are yours. Their opportunities are shared by all in your organization. It's your common ground.

Years ago, a member of the Salem Area Chamber of Commerce asked us to help them tell their story. The result was a couple of thirty-second television commercials in which they told the story of why they give to causes which benefit teachers and students in the classroom. The emotional impact of these stories was great. I remember saying, "If this process didn't cost almost $4,000, we'd do more of them."

The cost of video has gone down so much that I've had to come through on that statement.

With my trusty Kodak Zi8 video camera (around a hundred bucks), a lavaliere microphone, some halogen shop lights from the home improvement store, and a $300 video editor (I use Camtasia Studio), we will endeavor to produce stories that humanize our organization. Picture a video testimonial shot in the style of your favorite interview from *60 Minutes*. In the end, viewers may wonder if we're promoting ourselves or our members. Perfect.

## Raise Your Finger

*If you don't tell your story, they will make one up about you.* The stories of your membership organization are being told by your members, or by former members you have failed.

Clinging to yesterday's agenda is killing your organization's future, little by little. The longer you take to make a change, the greater the risk of having a *United Airlines moment* caused by an antiquated value proposition.

The remarkable nature of your membership organization lies in the stories your members tell about why they exist. Within these stories are why they are a member of tomorrow's membership organization.

I refuse to sit and wish for more media, more attention, or more advertising dollars. Refuse with me. The clock is ticking.

This manifesto exists because I'm seeking people who want to shake things up with me. People like Amanda Pasdon and Jim Butler and Stephanie Kirksey and Mike Varney.

And Steve Millard in Cleveland, Doug Holman in San Diego, Bob Thomas in Lansing, Scott Ashton in Oceanside, Tim Giuliani in Tallahassee, Brian Willms in Loveland, Ben Quintana in Boise and Aaron Nelson in Chapel Hill.

What got you here won't get you there. Tell a new story for your organization. Put your members in your story. Act like their agent, because you are.

If you find that you are worried about the future of your organization, perhaps it is because you are not doing anything about it.

The story of tomorrow's membership organization starts today. Let's re-do membership. Raise a finger. Let's go.

# Acknowledgements

So many thanks... To **Mom** for your eternal support and encouragement. To my brothers **Britt** and **Troy** for being so disciplined, and showing me the way. To my **Dad** for planting business in my head when I was 12.

To my other family, my teammates at the **Salem Area Chamber of Commerce** (current and past): Sylvia Forster, Sharron Seideman, Rita Rasmussen, Carole Reynolds, Cori Pratt, Jason Brandt, Kathy Moore, Jessica Chambers, Tonya Valentine, Chandra Andersen, Lisa Franceschi-Campbell, Kim Leighty, Tracey Etzel, Susie Ingersoll, Chris McLaran and Myron Musick. You inspire me and keep me grounded. All-stars, every single one of you.

To **Mike Varney** for challenging my reality. To **Shane Moody** for being untouchable and accessible at the same time. To **Troy McLellan** for keeping me focused when I was frustrated. To **Matt Pivarnik** for setting the bar even higher right before it was my turn to jump. To **Doug Holman** for always speaking the truth about this business, and for being great at what you do. To **Ben Wolf** for participating in my brainstorms. To **Kate Volman** for the phone calls you thought were just for you. To **Amanda Pasdon** for your endless encouragement. To **Dawn Moliterno** for helping me make sense of memberships. To **Steve Millard** for pushing the industry and wearing more hats than I thought possible.

To **Mick Fleming** for your steady hand and voice. To **Dave Kilby** for having high standards and forcing me to keep my research fresh. To **Ray Langen** for sharing his love for the people side of this business. To **Keith Woods** for showing me that research can be fun. To **Paula Creekmore** for the sales training I use nearly every day, even in non-sales endeavors. To **Cameron Herold** for 6 months of business training that will last a lifetime. To **Alan Corder** for giving me a shot.

To **Mike McLaran** for, well, everything... not the least of which is your hunch on hiring day.

To **Jennifer Powers** and **Tim Fahndrich** for 52 Thursday afternoons. To **Shaun Lumachi** for pushing constantly. To **Tom Hoffert** for that one day when you were the difference, and every day since.

And to **Seth Godin** for helping me find my voice, and putting into plain English what had been on the tip of my tongue for years.

# About the Author

Kyle Sexton is an award-winning marketing strategist and international speaker on the topics of membership development, marketing and technology. As the founder of *Fast Chamber*, a business development firm specializing in membership organizations, he was recognized by *Chamber Executive* magazine as one of the most influential innovators in his industry.

Kyle is the chamber of commerce industry's foremost authority on membership tiers, and coaches organizations through their transition from a traditional dues method to a progressive tiered-investment model.

As director of member services for the Salem Area Chamber of Commerce, Kyle was recognized as the 2007 Chamber Staff Person of the Year by the Western Association of Chamber Executives. He now works as the director of business development for the Salem Chamber, with a focus on innovative services for the region's small businesses.

Kyle's work on SalemChamber.org propelled the site to be the top-ranked local or regional chamber of commerce site on the web, as measured by Alexa.com. His innovations have been featured in *The Wall Street*

*Journal, Business On Main* from MSN, and smSmallBiz.com from *Smart Money*.

In 2008, he created what is now ChamberPeople.com, the web's largest social network exclusive to chambers of commerce. He is also the creator of the Chamber SalesEngine, an automated online membership sales module and lead-generator for chambers of commerce.

*Photo by Steve Snyder*

At age 33, Kyle was one of the youngest members of the Board of Directors of The American Chamber of Commerce Executives. He also served ACCE as Chair of the Membership Development Advisory Board. He is a Lifetime Achievement Award recipient from ACCE's

Circle of Champions sales division with over 1,000 memberships sold.

He serves as faculty for the Western Association of Chamber Executives (WACE) Academy, as well the United States Chamber of Commerce Institute of Organizational Management.

*Fast Chamber* develops franchise-quality membership development systems for chambers of commerce. His research and methods have been featured in industry publications, as well as national conventions and regional conferences.

He has been marketing and selling memberships since 1996. Prior to working for in the association industry, he was the Director of Marketing & Corporate Services for a chain of Gold's Gym locations in Western Oregon. His work was honored with the 2001 Gold's Gym International Award for Outstanding Advertising from among 600 franchises worldwide.

Kyle received the 1994 Pioneer Award for his first business venture, a College Pro Home Painters franchise which he operated for 2 years while attending the University of Oregon.

Kyle sings some mean karaoke and lives in Salem, Oregon, with his son, Wyatt.

# Bibliography

These are the books that inspired or are referenced in this one, and some others you should read, in no particular order.

*Linchpin – Are You Indispensable*, by Seth Godin
Godin describes this book as his life's work, and scared the hell out of me when he said it would be his last book. What he meant is that it was to be his last book from a traditional publisher. *Linchpin* describes the traits required in order to get away from being a replaceable cog in someone else's system, and moving into the artful work that matters.

*Made to Stick*, by Chip Heath and Dan Heath
The Heath brothers do their homework. The revelations I had while reading this book really helped me to understand why my strategies and practices work.

*The Purple Cow*, by Seth Godin
I've had more people thank me for recommending this book than any other. If you want to know how to move away from conventional advertising and turn your business into pure marketing, read this book. I've read it at least 18 times.

*Little Teal Book of Trust – How to Earn it, Grow it, and Keep it to Become a Trusted Advisor in Sales, Business & Life*, by Jeffrey Gitomer
Whether you've lost it or you're looking to keep it, Jeffrey simplifies a very tender topic. To put trust into business terms is invaluable.

*Poke the Box*, by Seth Godin
This is the first book from Godin's Domino Project, a mostly digital publishing venture with Amazon. Brilliant. I highlighted more lines in this work than any other, ever.

*How to Nail Voice Mail*, by Shawna Schuh
Shawna teaches you how to behave like someone who wants to be invited back to dinner, or to a dinner meeting. It's not just about voice mail; it's about business communications.

*Tribes – We Need You to Lead Us*, by Seth Godin
You can probably insert the name of your membership organization each time Godin uses the word *tribes* in this work.

*Double Double – How to Double Your Revenue and Profit in 3 Years or Less*, by Cameron Herold
Cameron was one of my first business mentors. Reading this book was like reading my mind – because he put all of these ideas in there in the first place.

*Permission Marketing – Turning Strangers into Friends, and Friends into Customers*, by Seth Godin
This map still works 12 years after it was written about email marketing. Read it, and apply it to social media, and a million other places where we give or ask for permission.

*Getting Things Done – The Art of Stress-Free Productivity*, by David Allen
No-nonsense advice to help you become more productive. I wonder if my book could have been completed without David's.

*Oh, Shift! How to Change Your Life with One Little Letter*, by Jennifer Powers
You could read this book at a poetry jam and win the crowd and the crown. Jennifer's raw and real style make for a beautiful read.

*The Dip – A Little Book That Teaches You When to Quit (and When to Stick)*, by Seth Godin
My least favorite of Godin's book, but only because of what it exposed in me. The Dip is all about work... you know, the hard part. I learned a lot, like sometimes, quitting is winning.

*The 4 Hour Work Week – Escape 9-5, Live Anywhere and Join the New Rich*, by Timothy Ferriss
This book starts out with motivation and inspiration and ends with a map. There are some very detailed how-to's in here, but the best part of Ferriss' book is the breaking of the glass ceiling over your cubicle.

*Mind Capture – How to Awaken Your Entrepreneurial Genius in a Time of Great Economic Change*, by Tony Rubleski
Tony will tell you he's in the reminding business, and his book reminded me of some very helpful strategies to make an impact with my work.

*Book Yourself Solid*, by Michael Port
Get unstuck with this workbook and reference guide. It's a must for any solo-preneur who wants to get it right instead of re-do it.

*Crush It! – Why Now is the Time to Cash in on Your Passion*, by Gary Vaynerchuk
A very personal piece from someone who dug deep into a niche to create a personal brand, a la Tim Ferriss.

*The Trust Edge – Transform Your Relationships, Revenue, and Results*, by David Horsager
David Horsager is a terrific presenter, and his book is a Bible for anyone playing a leadership role in the lives of others, be it professional or personal.

*Can I Have 5 Minutes of Your Time*, by Hal Becker
I met Hal in Toronto in 2001, and his sales philosophy became my marketing philosophy: "I'm independently wealthy and I don't need your business." Have confidence in your business strategy. I love Hal's work.

*Go For No*, by Richard Fenton and Andrea Waltz
In a world inundated with books on techniques for getting to yes, Richard Fenton & Andrea Waltz recommend just the opposite. Andrea and Richard are knowledgeable and inspiring.

Sandler Sales Institute: Hungerford, Creekmore & Company
Paula Creekmore and Dennis Hungerford
Eugene, Oregon | 541-686-0993 | hcc.sandler.com